Mia's Boxes of Love

by **Mia Clayton**

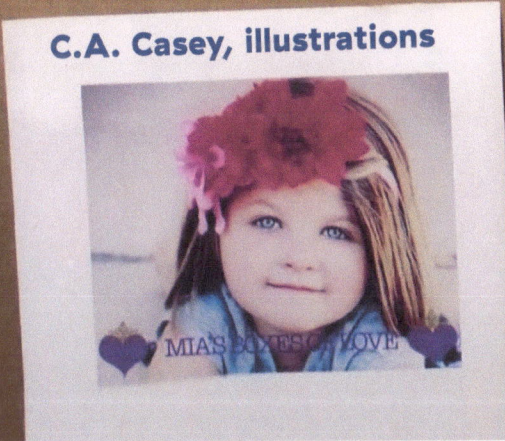

C.A. Casey, illustrations

One day we were driving

AND I SAW A HOMELESS PERSON ON THE SIDEWALK.

I talked to my mommy and daddy about people who don't have homes or families who can help them out.

It made me sad.

At home I started thinking about my favorite person in the whole world . . .

Kid President!

I have pretty much seen all of his videos.

In my favorite video he talks about treating everyone like it is their birthday.

THAT IS WHEN MIA'S BOXES OF LOVE STARTED.

My mommy and daddy talked to a homeless shelter called

FAMILY ASSISTANCE PROGRAM

and we started to collect the things that they needed.

The first things we collected were backpacks, lunch pails, and all kinds of other school supplies.

School was going to be starting soon and we wanted everyone to start the year off prepared.

EVERY OCTOBER, KID PRESIDENT DOES SOMETHING CALLED "SOCKTOBER."

During the month of October you get new socks and donate them to your local homeless shelter.

I wanted to do Socktober, so at my school I started collecting socks in a big sock box.

In our boxes we included many of the most needed items.

MOST SHELTERS NEVER HAVE ENOUGH SOCKS, UNDERWEAR OR DIAPERS.

We try to help as many people as we can and do fundraisers (that's a big word for raising money) a couple times of year.

EACH YEAR WE DONATE MORE AND MORE SOCKS AND MORE KIDS LEARN ABOUT HELPING OTHERS.

I have lots of pictures of me with socks.

My favorite part of Socktober other than helping people, is to make **a big pile of socks** and jump in it.

HAVING A NON-PROFIT TAKES WORK.

My mommy and daddy had to fill out paperwork, whatever that is. They showed me the pile of papers and it was huge.

WE ALSO HAVE TO HAVE MONTHLY MEETING, BUT I AM THE BOSS SO I AM IN CHARGE.

The BOSS

We mostly talk about the next fundraiser we are going to do or the next volunteer event.

I have so many awesome toys, books and movies. I just want other people to feel as happy as I do.

There are bad things that happen in the world but I want to be part of the good in the world.

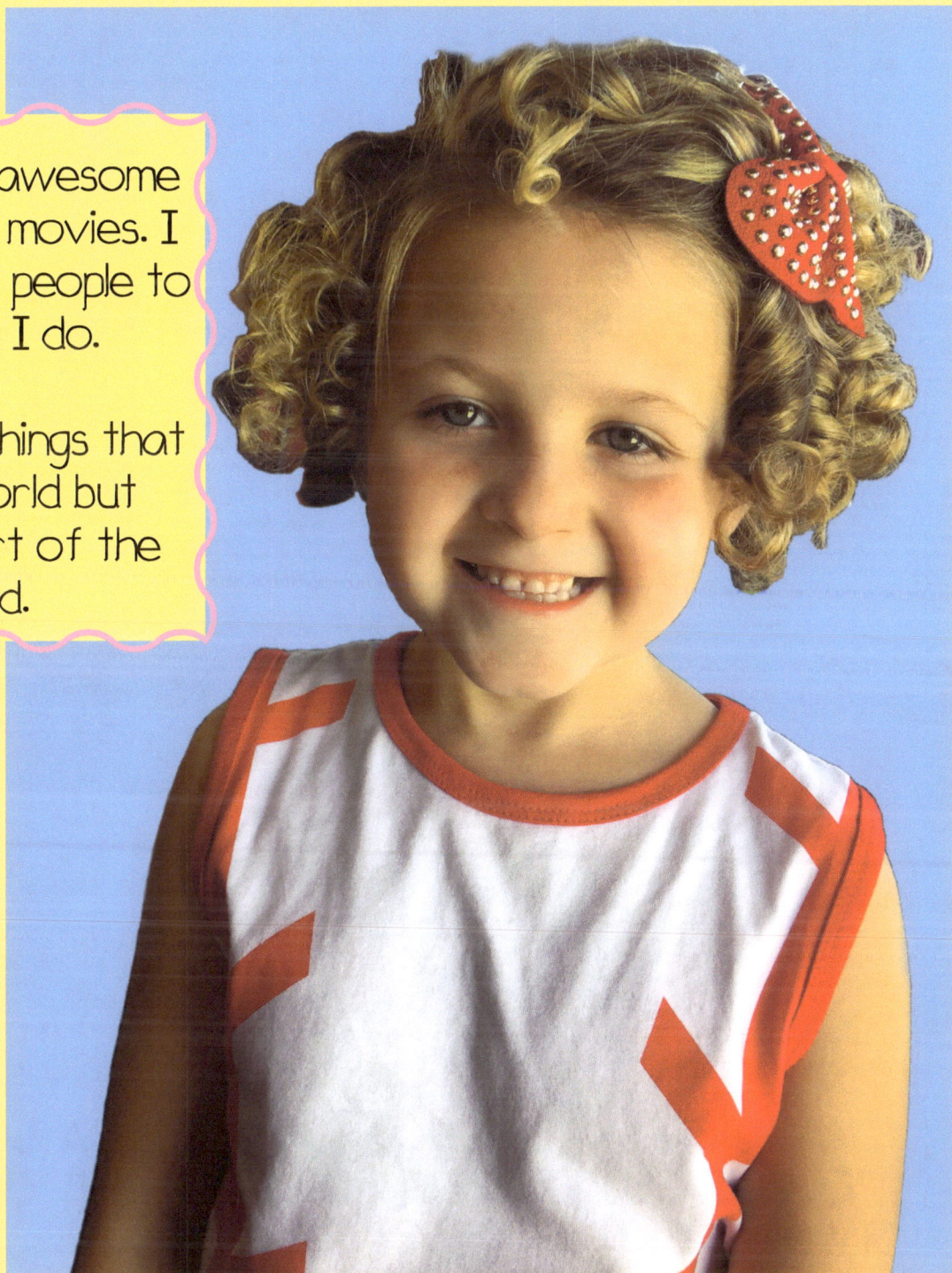

The best part about helping people is knowing that I am changing the world.

I am just one person and I am able to help so many.

IMAGINE WHAT WOULD HAPPEN IF A LOT OF PEOPLE GOT TOGETHER. I BET WE COULD HELP TWO MILLION PEOPLE!

IT'S IMPORTANT FOR KIDS TO KNOW THAT WHAT THEY THINK MATTERS.

ANYONE CAN MAKE THEIR DREAMS COME TRUE

IF THEY WORK HARD ENOUGH AND IF ADULTS BELIEVE IN THEM.

Mia's Boxes of Love, Inc.

Nonprofit 501(c)(3) Charity
(708) 782-6436

"It is my dream to change the world."

miasboxesoflove.org

Facebook: Mia's Boxes of Love
Twitter: #MiasBoxesofLove
Instagram: miasboxesoflove

My ultimate dream is to have my own place where homeless people can live and I can take care of them.

I KNOW THAT I CAN CHANGE THE WORLD JUST BY BEING ME. I KNOW THAT YOU CAN, TOO!

978-1-949290-33-2 paperback

Cover Design
by

Sappling
Studio

A Dragonfeather Book

Dragonfeather Books
a division of
Bedazzled Ink Publishing Company
Fairfield, California
http://www.bedazzledink.com

visit http://miasboxesoflove.org to learn more about Mia's Boxes of Love